to

How to Write an Essay

by Jonny Patrick

Contents

About this book

> *Meanwhile, you will write an essay on 'Self-indulgence'. There will be a prize of half a crown for the longest essay, irrespective of any possible merit.*
> **Evelyn Waugh, *Decline and Fall***

I don't remember when I first heard the word 'essay'. Perhaps it was in the late 1970s. At the time my own homework consisted of spelling lists and making things with pipe cleaners, but my older brother was always grumbling about things called 'essays'. It wasn't long before I was grumbling about them myself, and ever since my life has been punctuated by them – writing them, reading them, setting them, marking them.

In Britain at least, you won't get through school without having to write an essay. Essays loom large in young lives, then, eventually, at the end of our teens or in our early twenties, they disappear, like exams, quietly and unmourned.

For the purposes of this book, an essay is a writing task set to students in a school or university. It may be a piece of coursework, a weekly tutorial essay, a term paper, a dissertation or an essay produced in a time-limited exam. As I am a teacher and examiner of English, the focus of this book is English literature. I hope, however, you will find the advice given here helpful in writing about other subjects too.

Some of that advice may contradict what you have been taught or, if you are a teacher, what you teach. That's fine. While you may disagree with me at least this book will make you think about your approach. And that in itself can only be helpful.

Chapter One: The Question

> *FRANK: In response to the question, 'Suggest how you would resolve the staging difficulties inherent in a production of Ibsen's Peer Gynt', you have written, quote, 'Do it on the radio', unquote.*
> Willy Russell, *Educating Rita*

My friend the question

Teachers tend to say the same things over and over again. Some of the students to whom they say the same things over and over again go on to become teachers. And so the catchphrase of one of my teachers has become my own: *'answer the* [insert expletive of choice] *question'*. There is much to be said for challenging received wisdom, but this particularly piece of received wisdom has persisted because it's the best piece of advice on essay-writing there is. So if you take one message from this book, let it be: *answer the question*.

Answering the question should be the starting point of your thinking and the focus of every word and sentence of the essay.

What *is* an essay question? It's somewhere

between an invitation, a prompt and an order:

- It's an **invitation** because it's offering you the opportunity to show what you know and what you can do;

- It's a **prompt** because the person setting it is giving you the cue to get going;

- It's an **order** because, ultimately, you're being asked for something specific.

Let's start by clarifying a couple of things. In a tennis match, you try your best to make it as difficult as possible for your opponent to return your shot. Setting essays is not like that at all. A good question-setter *wants* you to be able to answer, fully and well. Secondly, the examiner has set this particular question because valuable and interesting things can be said in response to it.

So the question is not there to trip you up. It is not a dastardly trap laid by a twisted, sadistic individual who longs to watch you fail. It's the biggest single aid you've got to writing a good essay. It helps you to structure your answer, as many questions invite or even imply a certain structure of argument, as we'll see below. It's best to think of the question not as an obstacle but as your *friend*. And like a good friend, it needs to be embraced and constantly in your thoughts.

Answering the question

FRANK: [...] There is a way of answering examination questions that is expected. It's a sort of accepted ritual, it's a game, with rules. And you must observe those rules. (He leans with one hand on the back of RITA's chair.) When I was at university there was a student taking his final theology exam. He walked into the examination hall, took out his pen and wrote 'God Knows all the answers', then he handed in his paper and left.

RITA: (impressed) Did he?

FRANK: When his paper was returned to him, his professor had written on it, 'And God gives out the marks'.

RITA: Did he fail?

FRANK: (breaking away slightly): Of course he failed. You see, a clever answer is not necessarily the correct answer.

Willy Russell, *Educating Rita*

If it is so obvious that you have to answer the question, why do so many students fail to do so? It's not because they haven't prepared and revised. On the contrary. In my experience, students are most likely to fail to answer the question when they *have* revised carefully.

Let's imagine that Claire knows all about the role of Lucio in *Measure for Measure* and wrote a good essay on it a year ago. In the exam, however, Claire is out of luck: 'her' question doesn't 'come up' and she isn't asked about Lucio but about the relationship between Isabella and the Duke. Claire knows about this, and if she gives it a few minutes' thought and planning can produce a fine essay on it. But no – she really wants to write about Lucio. She's memorised ten quotations about him and three really long ones from an article she found online. What a shame that all this should go to waste!

So she writes, and writes well, about Lucio. But she wasn't invited, prompted or ordered to write about Lucio. And so poor Claire can't receive the high marks she perhaps deserves.

At worst, a failure to answer the question can come across as a wilful refusal to engage with an instruction; most often, however, it suggests a timidity, a lack of confidence in your own ability to think new things or to think in new ways about what you already know. An examiner knows this, but ultimately has to be tough. If you don't answer the question, you're not doing your job. If you went to a restaurant and ordered fish and the waiter brought you ice-cream, you'd be disappointed, however much you like ice-cream and however good the ice-cream might be.

Questioning the question

Once I'd got into the way of turning a question on its head... I began to get pleasure out of the technique itself... sketching out skeleton answers to all sorts of questions and using the same facts,

for instance, to argue opposite points of view, all
seasoned with a wide variety of references and
quotations. I knew it wasn't scholarship, and in
the Final Honours schools it would only take me
so far, but it was my only hope.

Alan Bennett, 'Introduction' to *The History Boys*

Let's imagine you've been set an essay question.
Write it down in full in the middle of a piece of
paper. You may prefer to plan on a screen but at this
stage pen and paper give you more flexibility. You
can jot things down, cross them out, join words or
phrases with lines or arrows.

**Once you've written down the question,
you're going to question it.** This will help to form
an initial spider-diagram of ideas; it won't be an
essay plan and you'll struggle to write a good essay
based on it alone. It's merely stage one.

The first question to ask is: *what format does the
question take?* Once you've identified that, other
useful questions follow.

The precise wording will vary, but you will
probably find that your question follows one of
these formats:

1. Questions that offer a judgment on a text or character and ask you to comment on that judgment

These questions will offer a critical view (often in
quotation marks, though usually devised by the

examiner rather than taken directly from a critic) and invite you to respond to and evaluate it. Here are a few examples:

> *'More a victim of his own arrogance than of political plotting.' How far do you agree with this view of the character of Coriolanus?*

> *'Heaney's poetry shies away from direct political statement.' How far do you agree with this statement?*

> *'Good writing about sexual relationships is invariably moral.' How far does your reading of any two texts lead you to agree with this statement?*

Alternatively, these questions may paraphrase an idea rather than use a direct quotation:

> *Explore the idea that* A Midsummer Night's Dream *is essentially a movement between order and chaos.*

> *Explore the idea that Ruth is the only truly powerful figure in* The Homecoming.

> *To what extent do you agree that the search for a home is central to modern American literature?*

In many ways, these are the most straightforward

questions to answer as they offer a perspective on the text or character that you can immediately question: does it match your own reading of the play or character? Are there nuances that you feel that the judgment overlooks? Such questions lend themselves very well to a **for-and-against** structure.

A useful way to begin to think about this type of question is to ask yourself the following questions:

a) why might someone believe this statement?

b) why might someone disagree with this statement?

Let's take an example, using a text that you may know.

> *In Romeo and Juliet, there is an unbridgeable gap between the younger and older generations.*

Why might someone believe this statement?

- The play constantly emphasises the difference between the older and younger generations. Younger characters such as Romeo, Tybalt and Mercutio are constantly seen in action, often violent action, whereas the older generation are seen as less athletic and energetic. (e.g. Lady Capulet mocks Capulet's request for his 'long sword', suggesting that a crutch would be more appropriate.)

- The first time we see Romeo he is a mystery to his mother and father, to the extent that they do not know where he is and quiz his cousin Benvolio to find out the source of his melancholy.

- Juliet's parents seem incapable of understanding her: her mother calls the nurse to remain with them in Act 1, Scene 2, as if she is uncomfortable being alone with her daughter. Juliet lies successfully to both of her parents, to the extent of convincing them that she is dead.

- Juliet's soliloquies suggest her isolation and the distance that separates her from her parents.

Why might someone disagree with this statement?

- The Nurse is a member of the older generation and her relationship with Juliet is one of the most intimate in the play (though they become more distant after Act 4).

- Friar Laurence is clearly a member of the older generation, yet he offers friendship, wise counsel and support to both Romeo and Juliet. Just as the Nurse is a kind of surrogate mother to Juliet, so Laurence is a kind of surrogate father to Romeo (Romeo's first line to him is 'Good morrow, father').

- Capulet is not always a tyrannical father to Juliet. When Paris first approaches him with a view to marrying Juliet, he is considerate of her wishes and her youth. Shakespeare does not present parents and children as implacable enemies; the gap between the generations is not unbridgeable.

Already, we can see that by asking these two key questions, we have the skeleton of a for-and-against argument. Test this method out by asking the two questions of a statement-based question on one of the texts that you are studying.

2. Questions that ask you to explore the ways in which a theme is presented

This is perhaps the most common form of question. It identifies a theme that the examiner recognises to be important to the text and asks you to think about the significance of the theme and *how* the writer explores it.

Consider some of the ways in which domestic space is explored in Plath's poetry.

Discuss Webster's presentation of death and dying in The Duchess of Malfi.

Consider the significance of the farm in modern South African literature.

These questions are trickier than questions which offer you a critical view or judgment. They don't offer a ready-made reading of the text which you can test and interrogate. You've got to do a little more work.

If we're not careful, we can end up just providing a rather monotonous list or catalogue of, say, ways in which characters die in *The Duchess of Malfi* rather than a close examination of *how* death and dying are presented and what the significance of death is in the play.

When faced with a 'theme' question, try to think about it from the outset in multiple ways. It's likely that the theme will seem to be particularly important to one particular character or moment, but we can open up further possibilities by considering other, less immediately obvious possibilities.

For example, a question on kingship in *Richard II* will prompt us to think immediately about the figure of Richard. But how might our argument develop if we remember that Richard is not the only king we see in the play? What about Bolingbroke? Or even the idealised figure of Richard's 'grandsire' Edward III, whom we never see but to whom a number of characters allude?

Or we might try to think from the outset about *different* ways in which a theme is presented, with a view to moving towards an eventual multi-phase 'for and against' structure. For example, we might ask ourselves about how domestic spaces in Plath are seen as threatening but equally how they are seen as protective and comforting.

3. Questions that ask you to explore the presentation and significance of a particular character or relationship

Discuss Hartley's presentation of Leo's relationships with Ted Burgess and Lord Trimingham in The Go-Between.

How does Beckett suggest the tensions between Hamm and Clov in Endgame?

How does Austen's writing make Henry Tilney such an appealing character in Northanger Abbey?

Although character-based criticism fell from favour long ago in academic circles, character-and-relationship-based essay questions remain popular, especially in schools. However sophisticated we later claim to be, most of us first have our interest in literature fired by the complexity and charisma of characters and by the fireworks between them. Teachers and examiners know this.

In answering such questions, it's important to remember that literary characters, however compelling, aren't real people and mustn't be discussed as if they are. Students are understandably seduced by Heathcliff's charm, or fired with indignation at the insults and degradation that he suffers, moved by Shylock's love for his daughter and appalled by the abuse heaped upon him, but we need to remember when writing about a text that we only feel these things because of decisions that a writer has made, decisions about structure, language, form and genre. It's for this reason that good character questions still include a reference to the writer or the writer's 'presentation' of a character.

4. Questions that ask you to consider the use and effect of a particular technique

> *Consider the effects of Collins's use of multiple narrators in* The Woman in White.

> *Discuss some of the ways in which Pope uses the heroic couplet* in The Rape of the Lock.

> *Discuss Williams's use of musical and lighting effects in* A Streetcar Named Desire.

It's less common to find questions like this, because they may seem to invite a dry, formalist approach, or lists of examples rather than an actual argument. They are still there in exam papers, however, and have the advantage of ensuring that the language, form and structure of a text will be central to a student's answer. In answering them, think about *effects*, i.e. how does the form the writer uses make a reader or audience feel and respond? How does a particular technique make us amused, or outraged, or surprised, or confused?

5. Questions that use a quotation from the text

Sometimes you will find that a quotation from the text is used in the question.

This is not strictly speaking a separate category of question, as a quotation will usually be followed by a prompt question which identifies it as one of the four types of question we have already examined. Here are some examples, with the categories to which they belong:

> *'Lord Darlington wasn't a bad man. He wasn't a bad man at all'. Consider the significance of this statement for the presentation of Lord Darlington in* The Remains of the Day.

– questions that offer a judgment on a text or character and ask you to comment on that judgment

> 'Religion used to try,/That vast, moth-eaten musical brocade/Created to pretend we never die'. In the light of this statement, discuss Larkin's presentation of religious practice and experience.

– questions that ask you to explore the ways in which a theme is presented)

> *'I think he only loves the world for him.'*

*Discuss the significance of the relationship of
Antonio and Bassanio in* The Merchant of Venice.

– questions that ask you to explore the presentation
and significance of a particular character or
relationship

*'In truth the prison unto which we doom
Ourselves no prison is: and hence for me,
In sundry moods, 'twas pastime to be bound
Within the Sonnet's scanty plot of ground...'*

*In the light of these lines, consider Wordsworth's
use of the sonnet form.*

– questions that ask you to consider the use and
effect of a particular technique

What's most important in this style of question is to
use the quotation. It's been chosen to help you. It
may even give you the outlines of a structure for
your essay. When presented with a quotation in the
question, always start by locating it:

• **Where does this phrase appear?** If it's a
description of a character and from early in the
text, is what it says still true by the end of the
play? In the first act of Othello, for example, the
Duke calls him "valiant", but by the end of the
play we might have good reason to question this
judgement.

- **Who says it and about whom?** It's important to be clear who is speaking in the quotation. Is it a character whose opinion we can and should trust? To take another example from Othello, the Moor describes himself as 'one that loved not wisely but too well' but makes this self-exculpatory judgment at the end of the play, when his downfall is complete and he is attempting to extract some dignity from his personal ruin. Literary characters – like the people we know – are rarely great judges of themselves and have a capacity for self-deception, so we should be wary of believing what they say about themselves. Similarly, we should be wary of what other characters say about them: love, hatred, political expediency or personal rivalry may have clouded their judgement.

- **Finally, ask yourself if you agree with the quotation.** Why might someone agree with it? Why not? As we've seen, asking these questions can take us a long way towards the development of a for-and-against essay structure.

Locating a quotation is essential yet it is remarkable how rarely students bother to do it. If the question is based on a quotation, it's often a great idea to start with it, locate it in the text and discuss its implications.

6. Questions that ask you about a specific poem or passage

We'll discuss these separately later – in chapter seven.

Definitions

Most exam questions are designed to be as clear and unambiguous as possible and examiners give considerable thought to the wording of their questions to make sure this is the case. (The same is not always true at university: I still recall being faced by a question which invited me to consider 'the epistemological function of metaphor in Proust' and wondering what on earth 'epistemological' meant.)

Nevertheless, some essay questions pivot on a key term that needs to be defined. So make sure that from the start that you are sure – in your own mind at least – what a key word in the question means or is going to mean in your essay. It's unlikely to be a word you've never heard before but it's still worth clarifying and defining exactly what it means.

Let's imagine we're answering the following question:

> *'Families in* King Lear *heal and harm in equal measure'*

We don't need to define every term: we all know what 'families' are. But it might be worth stopping to think about 'heal' and 'harm'. 'To heal' means to cure, to make better, both physically, mentally and morally. How many of these meanings are appropriate to *King Lear*? Lear's daughter Cordelia presides over his 'recovery' in Act IV and perhaps acts as agent of his moral regeneration. But is Cordelia 'family' or just a loving individual? Edgar helps to 'heal' his father Gloucester of his suicidal urges in Act IV but when he reveals his true identity as Gloucester's son, the shock kills the old man.

'To harm' means to damage physically, morally and spiritually, and we can doubtless think of numerous examples of dysfunctional families that harm individuals in *Lear*: the generation that includes Cordelia, Regan, Goneril, Edgar and Edmund are all arguably victims of the institution of family, of family law and/or abusive family relationships.

But we could be more flexible in our reading of the question: can families heal and harm a *state*, for instance? Lear arguably sacrifices his nation and its people in a botched attempt to avoid family tensions. If family interests inevitably harm national interests, does the play imply that hereditary monarchy is ultimately flawed? '[I]n equal measure' is a crucial phrase too: it suggests there is a balance between hurting and healing, that families do *as much* harm as good. Such a phrase invites challenge: ultimately, we might decide to argue that families do more good than harm and that the play seems to demand a modification of the institution of the family rather than its destruction.

Some of this work of definition will be done for your own purposes as you plan the essay. But you may feel that one or more terms in the question are so ambiguous and/or essential that you need to define them *explicitly* in your introduction. So if answering the question 'To what extent can *Moby-Dick* be seen as a study in tyranny?', it would be a good idea to begin your introduction with a clear and crisp definition of the key term 'tyranny'.

You may have noticed that I defined the key word 'essay' in my introduction to this book. The obvious source of definitions is the *Oxford English Dictionary* (*OED*). Have a look at it if you can. Better still, formulate and set out your own, informed definition, stating what the key word or words are going to mean for the purposes of *your* essay. And please, please don't start with a definition from Wikipedia.

Chapter Two: Planning

"A mighty maze! But not without a plan."
Alexander Pope, *Essay on Man,* **Epistle I**

Let's take a moment to re-cap. If you've followed the instructions in Chapter Two, you've gone through the first stage of writing an essay. You've scrutinised and questioned the question. You have a piece of paper with the question written in the middle of it. Ideally, asking questions about the question has produced ideas that you've been able to add to the piece of paper.

Forming a constellation around the question will be brief annotations:

- maybe definitions of terms in the question;

- maybe a section listing reasons why someone might agree with an idea and another listing why someone might not;

- maybe a section about how the question could be answered differently about different characters.

You may well have drawn lines and arrows to connect similar ideas; perhaps you've underlined or drawn a circle around key ideas or produced a spider diagram with the question at the centre. The essay-writing process is well under way.

It's tempting at this stage, especially if you're

under time pressure, to start writing, perhaps using the different 'spokes' of a spider diagram or groups of similar ideas as your paragraphs. If feeling this temptation, resist it. What is in front of you is *not* an essay plan. It's a first phase, a set of ideas and observations that are reasonably well developed and potentially exciting, but not yet organised enough to be the basis for a concise and persuasive essay. What you are looking at is not an essay plan because:

- there's no introduction or conclusion;
- there are unlikely to be detailed examples, quotations or sketches of textual analysis. As you were doing that initial thinking and scribbling, you may not even have had the text open;
- there's no clear sense of what logical sequence your ideas should be in.

You may worry that the clock is ticking, but remember – **spending time turning these initial thoughts into a coherent essay plan will actually save you time in the long run,** as it is likely to ensure that you write clearly, concisely, elegantly and economically, avoiding repetition, redundancy and self-contradiction.

What you're going to do now is produce an essay plan from which you can actually write. Rather than a sheet of paper with single words, arrows, lines and circles, it will be a sequential and linear document, probably in bullet points, indicating the content of your introduction, each separate paragraph and the conclusion.

It will include references to examples you're going to use: if you're working with the text, these examples don't need to be written out in full at this stage, just indicated by page number. If you're working without the text, they could just be shortened forms of quotations you know by heart.

Once this phase is complete, you know exactly what you're going to say, from the beginning of the introduction to the last word of the conclusion. Then you can begin to 'write up' the final essay.

Overall essay structure

Your essay needs to have a clear shape. Specifically, it needs an introduction, a main body and a conclusion.

The main body will be made up of a number of paragraphs marking different stages of the argument. It's impossible to specify how many paragraphs the main body should have as it will depend on the length of the essay and the structure of the argument. For the sake of convenience, many teachers tell students that the main body should be made up of three paragraphs, and that's not a bad guideline, especially at GCSE level or below. It can lead to a certain rigidity, though, as if three were indeed – as hip hop legends De La Soul once claimed – 'the Magic Number'. (Cue anguished cries of 'but

I don't have a third paragraph!' and/or third paragraphs that are made of padding or unconvincing arguments.)

Especially in longer essays, it's more useful to think in terms of three *phases* rather than three paragraphs, each phase of an argument being made up of as many paragraphs as it requires. But don't panic if your argument only seems to have two phases. Better a well-made two-phase argument than an essay where the third phase is made up of half-baked waffle.

For and against

One of the most effective essay structures is, as it has always been, the 'for and against'. It's an ancient form and it's stuck around for good reason. It has the benefits of simplicity, familiarity and clarity, and its adversarial nature tends to give drive to an essay. The fact that it involves consideration of more than one side of an argument also creates a sense of fairness and balance that prevents what you write from becoming a rant. Study published articles or speeches and you'll find a 'for and against' structure in most of them. I'm happy to admit that it's there in almost everything I've ever written.

The 'for and against' structure is particularly recommended if you're dealing with questions that offer a judgment on a text or character and ask you to comment on that judgment.

If you asked those two key questions

why might someone believe this statement?

and

why might someone disagree with this statement?

you will already have two 'sides' to your argument and will have written down some ideas to support each. You need to decide now which of the 'sides' you find more persuasive, because this will affect the shape of your 'for and against' structure; it may be an 'against and for'.

Deal with the side with which you don't ultimately agree first, followed by the side with which you do agree. In this way, your argument has more force as the reader comes last to the arguments you favour, and thus these arguments are freshest in the reader's mind after finishing your essay.

In Shakespeare's *Julius Caesar*, one of Brutus's fatal mistakes is to allow his adversary Mark Antony to speak *second* at Caesar's funeral. Brutus himself goes first and delivers a fine piece of oratory that the crowd laps up. But Antony has the advantage of going second: he now knows Brutus's arguments and can refute and indeed mock them. What's more, by the time Antony has finished speaking, Brutus's words have been forgotten and he has no chance to reply to Antony and correct his many distortions.

You should aim to devote more of your essay

to the arguments that you favour than to the arguments you don't. There's no need to be resolutely 'fair' in giving equal house-room and hearing to both sides, though it's intellectually dishonest to distort or oversimplify your opponents' arguments (even if everyone does it to some degree). So, if we are following a 3-paragraph/phase structure, the 'for and against' essay looks like this:

- Introduction
- Paragraph/phase 1: the 'other' side of the argument, with which you do not ultimately agree
- Paragraph/phase 2 and 3: the side of the argument with which you do ultimately agree
- Conclusion

Clearly, there will be an important pivot and transition between paragraph/phase 1 and paragraph/phase 2, which will need to be marked by a transitional connective such as 'However', 'Nevertheless', 'Despite this' in the topic sentence that begins paragraph/phase 2.

Other structures

Not all types of question, however, lend themselves readily to the 'for and against structure'. It's tailor-made for those questions that give you a judgement on a text or character and ask you how far you agree with it, but what about the questions that don't do that? These are the type of questions that we identified in Chapter Two as

Questions that ask you to explore the ways in which a theme is presented

Questions that ask you to explore the presentation and significance of a particular character or relationship

and

Questions that ask you to consider the use and effect of a particular technique

In the following examples, there's no opinion in quotations which we can hold up to our own judgement and use to build up a set of arguments 'for and against':

Discuss the ways in which Gaskell presents city life in North and South.

Explore Shakespeare's presentation of the relationship between Macbeth and Lady Macbeth.

Explore the effects of Selvon's use of West Indian dialect in The Lonely Londoners.

In fact, the 'for and against' structure *can* still be

used in answering these questions and it's always worth thinking about whether there is a way to view such questions as inviting a debate. Few great writers are crude enough to present a theme or idea in just one way.

For example, 'Discuss the ways in which Gaskell presents city life in *North and South*' might be answered by discussing the ways in which city life is presented as alienating and degrading, followed by a consideration of how Gaskell suggests that city life can also be stimulating and rejuvenating.

Similarly, the question 'Explore Shakespeare's presentation of the relationship between Macbeth and Lady Macbeth' could be approached through a weighing of two contrasting visions of their relationship: one that sees it as a loving and mutually supportive, the other that sees it as destructive and abusive.

The question 'Explore the effects of Selvon's use of West Indian dialect in *The Lonely Londoners*', however, doesn't lend itself so readily to such an approach. In theory, you could try to suggest that Selvon's novel stages some sort of debate over the status of West Indian Creoles, but it would be hard to argue that there is any sense in which the novel is 'against' Caribbean English.

If we try to impose a 'for and against' structure here, we risk distorting our thinking about a novel by trying to make it fit the straitjacket of a particular essay structure. The tail is in danger of wagging the dog. We need to look for a different structure.

At the stage of 'questioning the question', you must decide whether your question needs an approach that is more *expository* than *argumentative*. By 'expository', I mean *showing and explaining* certain aspects of a text, rather than *persuading* your reader that it should be interpreted in a particular fashion.

The danger of the expository approach is that the resulting essay can have less argumentative edge, being more of a survey of the subject than the development of a reading. There is also a danger that the expository essay can become a bit of a browse around an issue, or a list of observations, rather than a proper overarching argument. On the other hand, it's less likely to become a rant and it allows you to consider a range of different and perhaps conflicting aspects of a text without having to force them into a coherent thesis.

Let's consider the following question:

Explore Shakespeare's presentation of betrayal in Othello.

There's not an obvious implicit 'for and against' structure in this question. It would be absurd to suggest that *Othello* is in any way a defence of betrayal or that betrayal is a 'good thing'. But a plodding answer to this question is simply going to list, in more or less detail, examples of betrayal in *Othello*. It's going to be a catalogue of betrayals, not a discussion of how Shakespeare approaches betrayal. It's likely to be long, boring to write and read and not sophisticated enough to earn a high grade.

Nevertheless, this style of question can produce excellent essays. Although we aren't going to use the 'for and against' structure, a good answer still has *to look at the question in more than one way*. So we should once again aim for a three-phase structure, ideally dealing with our least obvious – and thus most original – approach to the question last. We might structure an answer as follows:

1. Iago as the play's main traitor
    - betrayal of 'friends': Othello, Roderigo, Cassio
    - betrayal of his master and challenge that this presents to master-servant bonds
    - betrayal of his country

2. Betrayal by Othello
    - of his wife Desdemona
    - of Desdemona's father Brabantio
    - of his own cultural heritage
    - of himself

3. Betrayal by Emilia
    - betrayal of her mistress Desdemona by stealing the handkerchief
    - however, she atones for this act of betrayal through the act of betraying her husband at the end of the play. In this sense, Shakespeare

suggests that betrayal is not always reprehensible.

Here it's important to note that we have three phases and that they increase in complexity. The thinking becomes less obvious and more original as the essay progresses. It would be risky or even perverse to ignore Iago but the essay becomes more complex if we look at other characters too.

If you know the play, you can probably think of other less obvious traitors: arguably, the play's primal act of betrayal is by the apparently 'innocent' Desdemona, who marries Othello without her father's knowledge or permission. This approach to the question is character-based but we don't have to think solely in terms of character to develop a multi-faceted approach to a thematic question. For example, we could consider the same question by thinking of different types of betrayal, again moving from the most obvious to the least:

1. Betrayal of a friend
   • Iago's betrayals of Othello, Roderigo, Cassio
   • Othello's betrayal of Brabantio
   • Cassio's refusal to betray his friend Othello (though ironically, he is accused and convicted of doing so)

2. Betrayal of a spouse
   • the play pivots on a suspected but entirely imaginary act of betrayal and infidelity as

Othello is convinced that his wife has betrayed him
- Iago is driven in part by a similarly illusory suspicion that his wife has betrayed him
- in order to expose her husband and bring him to justice, Emilia has to betray him at the end of the play

3. Betrayal of oneself
   - the play charts Othello's battle to learn the nature of his true self and to remain faithful to it. Iago tricks him into distrusting his true, loving, rational self, his 'free and open nature', to become a violent, jealous monster
   - Othello is arguably a kind of cultural traitor in that he has become the servant of a European power that suppresses cultural otherness
   - the use of soliloquies enables us to see where characters unconsciously betray their own desires through repetitions and slips

The approach here is not primarily character-led but rather involves three different ways of thinking about the theme of betrayal. Once again, we move from the most straightforward way of thinking about the question (the literal betrayal of a friend) to the most complex and original (a metaphorical betrayal of the self). And we're still working with an essay structure that involves an introduction, three paragraphs/phases and a conclusion.

Writing the plan

You're now ready to write a detailed plan. This is the engine-room of the essay writing process and it's where the really hard thinking happens. This plan is your detailed script for the final essay and you need to stick to it, so that when you come to the actual writing you can concentrate on your style rather than doing 'new' thinking.

Obviously, once in a while, as you're doing the final write-up, you'll notice new things or make a connection that you haven't seen before. It's fine to make slight deviations from and modifications and additions to the plan as you're writing but if this is going to lead to a major restructuring (e.g. a whole new paragraph), stop and return to the planning stage.

What does an essay plan look like? It depends on how much time you have. In an exam, you'll probably be spending no more than 10-15 minutes on it, so it won't have the level of detail you might be able to include in a plan for that you're writing at home. Nonetheless, it still needs to be clear and structured, so that you know exactly where you're going before you start writing.

Your plan will ideally be made up of a series of sections corresponding to the introduction, three paragraphs/phases and conclusion. I like to mark each of those sections with a sub-heading:

'Introduction', 'Paragraph 1', 'Paragraph 2', 'Paragraph 3', 'Conclusion' and a brief outline of what each paragraph is about.

Just a few words is enough. In the essay on *Othello* outlined above, the sub-headings for my sections would be 'Paragraph 1: Betrayal of a friend', 'Paragraph 2: Betrayal of a spouse', 'Paragraph 3: Betrayal of oneself'. If you have time, it's an excellent idea to write your topic sentences (the first sentence of each paragraph) in full at this planning stage.

Beneath the sub-heading of each paragraph/ phase, write a series of bullet points giving you a prompt about what exactly you're going to be arguing, including quotations, page references, dates etc. that you're going to need. These should be detailed enough to prompt you, but not full sentences. Sometimes one or two words will be enough.

Remember to plan your introduction and conclusion at this stage, in as much detail as any other part of the essay. Just writing 'Introduction' and 'Conclusion' is not sufficient. You need to be absolutely clear what is going to be in these vital sections of an essay before you write them.

The next three chapters give you more detail on how to build your introduction, paragraphs and conclusion.

The more carefully you plan at this stage, the better your final essay is likely to be. Yes, you have to watch the clock, but in my experience, carefully planned essays tend to be shorter, clearer and more economical. So always take time to plan.

Chapter Three:
The Introduction

"Then how should I begin?"
T.S. Eliot, 'The Love Song of J. Alfred Prufrock'

"The beginning is the most important part of any work, especially in the case of a young and tender thing; for that is the time at which the character is being formed and the desired impression is more readily taken."
Plato, *Republic*, Book II

Like every other part of your essay, the introduction must be planned. Just writing 'Intro' and underlining it is not a plan.

The introduction is probably the most important part of the essay, especially in exams. If you write a good one that wins the examiner over, and assures her or him that you

a) are answering the question
b) have some ideas and
c) know what you are going to be saying

you have gone a long way towards success. It's quite difficult – though not impossible – to 'lose' an examiner after writing a strong introduction.

When I am examining, a good introduction

makes me breathe a sigh of relief because it convinces me that what I'm going to read will be relevant to the question, that the student has something to say and that what follows will be coherent and directed towards a particular end-point. I very rarely see a good introduction to a weak essay. Introductions shouldn't be long: as a rough guide, half a side in average-sized handwriting is the maximum. An effective introduction can be as short as one sentence.

Before setting out what an introduction *should* do, let's look briefly at a few types of introduction that *don't* work:

No introduction at all: some essay writers just get stuck in, moving immediately into a great deal of detail and quotation. Provided the material is relevant, this can produce an acceptable essay but you're likely to bewilder your reader. An essay tends to be more persuasive if you say at once what it is setting out to prove. Without a clear introduction, this is not likely to become clear until some way into the essay, if at all.

Throat-clearing: some writers know you're supposed to *have* an introduction but not what an introduction should *do*. So they produce the equivalent of the uncertain public speaker's throat-clearing 'ahem'. Imagine the question is 'Discuss the ways in which family relationships are presented in Tony Harrison's poetry'. A throat-clearing introduction will go something like this:

Tony Harrison's poetry discusses family relationships in many different ways. He uses language to explore the ways in which family members relate to one another. Through the form of his poetry, we can see that family relationships are very important to Tony Harrison.

This at least has the merit of referring to the question and suggests the essay will be relevant. But it says nothing and feels simply like an attempt to defer the troublesome business of making an argument. As such, it's a waste of space and time. If all your introduction is doing is paraphrasing the question, why bother?

Showing off knowledge: students often have an impressive depth and breadth of knowledge. They have their favourite facts, quotations and ideas, painfully hewn or lovingly chiselled from the coalface of revision, and they are determined to use them. And where better to do a little knowledge-imparting than in an introduction? So we get something like this:

Born in Leeds in 1937, Tony Harrison is one of Britain's best-loved poets and has been described by playwright Harold Pinter (1930-2008) as having '[a] voracious appetite for language'. After studying Latin and Greek at Leeds Grammar School, he read Classics at the University of Leeds...

The writer here clearly knows a lot about Harrison, but makes absolutely no progress towards answering the question of how his poetry explores family relationships. Some of the biographical knowledge here *could* contribute productively to the argument: the writer doesn't – but might have – mentioned that the extent of Harrison's education put a strain on his family relationships by creating a gap in experience and expectations between himself and his working-class parents.

In answering this question, the key question of family relationships needs to be introduced first. All other material is subordinate. Irrelevant material (e.g. the quotation from Pinter, Pinter's dates) is just occupying space and time that could be used more productively.

Introductions that say what the essay is going to do: many students are taught that a good introduction states what the essay is *going* to do. Here's an example.

In this essay I will be discussing the ways in which Tony Harrison's poetry explores family relationships. Firstly, I will be examining the ways in which family relationships are seen as nurturing and tender. Next, the essay will look at the ways in which family relationships are seen as a source of pain and suffering. Finally, I will suggest that Harrison uses shifts and contrasts in register and diction to suggest the strains and tensions within his family unit.

There's much to praise in this: it's clear that the essay will be focused on the question and that the writer has a clear structure in mind. Though sometimes it's a little vague and non-committal ('the ways in which family relationships are seen as nurturing and tender' doesn't specify *how* the language, form and imagery of Harrison's poetry suggest nurture and tenderness), there is a promising focus on specific techniques in the writer's identification of 'shifts and contrasts of register and diction' as a way of suggesting and reflecting strains and tensions within the family.

But the future tense seems awkward to me. **Why waste time saying what you're going to do? Just get on and do it!**

Many teachers recommend starting an essay with a statement of what the essay will argue and indeed the first paragraph of many academic articles begin 'In this essay, I shall argue...' or 'This article will argue that...'

Well, it's a matter of personal taste, but I've always disliked meta-commentary like this within an essay – i.e. an essay that spends time talking about what it is going to do, is doing or has done. It's repetitive and, what's more, can feel self-important. Above all, it's a waste of time and space. Rather than saying 'In this essay I shall be arguing that Tony Harrison presents family relationships as a source of pain and suffering', why not say simply and confidently 'Tony Harrison presents family relationships as a source of pain and suffering'?

So what *should* an introduction do? Most importantly, it should answer the question. One of the major tasks of an introduction is to reassure the reader that the writer has understood the question and is definitely going to answer it, so that what follows will be entirely relevant. If it's an exam essay, your introduction should (implicitly) say to the examiner 'I am answering your question'. So begin with the question, using some of its terms in your first sentence.

If it's a question that involves a judgment or opinion on a text or character, start with a statement such as 'This statement implies that...' If there are terms that need defining, do it here. But above all give a clear and direct answer to the question in one or two sentences. So if asked to 'Discuss the ways in which family relationships are presented in Tony Harrison's poetry', it would be a good idea to begin the essay with a sentence that reads 'In Tony Harrison's poetry, family relationship are presented...'. The last example we had could thus be re-written as

> Tony Harrison's poetry presents family relationships as nurturing and tender, though they are also seen as a source of pain and suffering. Harrison uses shifts and contrasts in register and diction to suggest the strains and tensions within his family unit.

It's not the most elegant of openings, but it's much

more economical and punchy. We've moved from four sentences to two and so the cautious, plodding tone has gone. The reader is left in no doubt that the writer is on task and we have a clear notion of what the essay is going to be arguing.

Some might contend that setting out your main argument directly like this gives too much away at the start, leaving nothing up your sleeve with which to surprise the reader. That may be true but we're writing an essay, not performing a magic trick. The introduction that teases and tantalises us by trailing some grand revelation to be pulled from the hat on the last page is usually just another attempt to defer the moment where a writer must commit to an argument.

There are other things we can and sometimes should do in an introduction. If we're writing about a passage, the first sentence of the introduction is the place to set the passage in context, stating where in the text it comes from, what's happened just before, and how the passage will affect subsequent events.

An introduction can also be a good place to begin to draw in some contextual material, explaining why the issue in question was important to a particular writer at a particular historical moment. So the introduction to an essay on family relationships in Harrison could include some biographical detail on his family and why his early life might have made family relationships such a cause of concern.

Similarly, if asked about the way law is represented in Dickens's *Bleak House,* your introduction might state that one of Dickens's first jobs was as a legal clerk. An introduction needs to be economical, however, so keep such references brief. Above all, don't get into detailed quotation and textual analysis at this point; those can wait until the main body of the essay.

The introduction matters. Get it right, and you're well on the way to writing an essay that's clear, authoritative and organised. Take time to *plan* it before you begin to write.

Chapter Four – The topic sentence and the paragraph

"Never forget that if you don't hit a newspaper reader between the eyes with your first sentence, there is no need of writing a second one."
Arthur Brisbane (1864-1936), Editor of the *New York Herald*

The topic sentence

The topic sentence is the first sentence of a paragraph. It's also the most important sentence. Along with the introduction and conclusion, your

topic sentences are the most important in your essay.

Academic articles, especially in the sciences, often begin with an abstract, which is a short paragraph, often in italics, summarising the article that follows. The article might run to 30 pages or more; the abstract is just a few lines. I'm fond of abstracts and wish they were used more in the arts and humanities; they stop me wasting time reading long articles that say little.

Your topic sentence should act as the abstract for the paragraph that follows it, setting out the major idea or argument of the paragraph. It's like the label on a package, the subject line of an email or the agenda of a meeting: it tells you what to expect, what you've got to look forward to (or brace yourself for). Topic sentences also answer the question, directly and explicitly, so that if I read the first sentence of each paragraph of your essay I will have your full argument in synopsis form. **One of the first things I do when marking an essay is read the topic sentences.**

What you should do in topic sentences:

Answer the question directly: The topic sentence won't be your whole answer but it will be a significant part of it. So if you're asked about the ways in which a writer presents a certain theme or character, each topic sentence might summarise one of those ways. Imagine I'm writing an essay on 'How does Dickens's writing make Bounderby such a dislikeable character in *Hard Times*?' One of the topic sentences might read:

> Dickens makes Bounderby unattractive and dislikeable through his use of grotesque description of Bounderby's physical appearance, which reflects his inner, moral ugliness.

This topic sentence definitely answers the question. It's not my *whole* answer; in other paragraphs I'll look at his treatment of his mother and the way Dickens uses metaphors that link Bounderby to violent and destructive forces. But this topic sentence makes it clear that I see the emphasis on and exaggeration of Bounderby's physical grotesqueness as central to the repugnance the reader feels towards him. In the rest of the paragraph, I'll explain in detail how Dickens's caricature works, using two or three specific examples, to support the overarching idea expressed in the topic sentence.

Use some of the terms of the question: When I was at primary school, we played hide and seek. To stop it becoming boring, we invented a rule requiring each seeker to return to 'base' (a rusty metal rubbish bin) and touch it at least once every five minutes, without, of course, being seen by the seeker. It is a useful metaphor for the role of topic sentences in essays. Like us with our can, the essay-writer should return to the question at regular intervals. The topic sentence is the place where you 'touch base', demonstrating to an examiner that you are answering the question and providing a regular, reassuring reminder of the direction and purpose of your essay. In the example above I included the words 'Dickens', 'Bounderby' and, most importantly, 'dislikeable', all of which appear in the question. **Using one or two of the key words from the question in topic sentences is a simple way of making sure that the relevance of each of your paragraphs is clear.**

Give a clear idea of what the paragraph is about: everything in the paragraph that follows the topic sentence should support the idea expressed by it. Think of the paragraph as a platoon of soldiers; the topic sentence is the platoon commander. It's in charge and the rest of the paragraph is subordinate to it. After planning and writing a paragraph, read it back to yourself and ask if everything in it supports the idea expressed in the topic sentence. If it doesn't, lose it. It doesn't belong there.

What you shouldn't do in topic sentences:

Don't say nothing: Forgive the double negative. In the previous chapter, we discussed (with the emphasis on *dis*-sing) introductions that are nothing more than place-holders or throat-clearing exercises. The same is true of topic sentences. Some students know that topic sentences are important but make them so bland and vacuous that they add nothing to the argument. Thus we see phrases such as 'There are many ways in which Dickens makes us dislike Bounderby'; 'Dickens uses imagery, structure and form to make Bounderby a dislikeable character'; or (my favourite) 'Dickens uses language to make Bounderby dislikeable'. (Saying a writer uses language is like saying that a carpenter uses wood. What else is a writer going to use? Dance? A sledgehammer? Plasticine?)

Don't try to say too much: in your topic sentences, don't promise more than a paragraph can deliver. Don't offer a cornucopia of different ideas. And avoid lists of ideas that are too diverse and complex to fit into a single paragraph that is clear, coherent and succinct. If I write

> Dickens makes us dislike Bounderby through direct narratorial denunciations, using violent imagery to describe his voice and movements, and by showing his indifference to his own mother, which implies an alienation from natural forces and bonds

I'm pouring far too much into what has to be a fairly small pot. The topic sentence is over-long and confusing, so the same is likely to be true of the ensuing paragraph. If I manage to do all that I've promised, the paragraph is likely to be so long and dense my reader will get lost or, more likely, I'll conk out and never get round to supporting all the ideas

I've trailed.

So keep topic sentences simple and clear, ideally expressing just one idea. Make sure they aren't open to the accusation levelled at Maverick by Stinger in Top Gun: 'Son, your ego is writing cheques your body can't cash.'

Don't include quotation and analysis: the topic sentence is really just the headline of the paragraph. It shouldn't give the precise details of what, when, why and how. Those will be dealt with in the body of the paragraph. Don't use your topic sentence to quote or analyse the effects of individual words, phrases, technical effects and sounds.

Don't explain what the paragraph will do: a topic sentence says what the paragraph will prove; it shouldn't say what it is about to do. Don't say 'In this paragraph I will show that...' or 'Now we shall turn to consider...' or 'My next point is...' or 'This paragraph will argue...' Such phrases are superfluous and give an essay a staccato rhythm, implying that the writer has to pause for breath between stages, like an unfit man climbing a staircase. An essay should be one continuous argument, not a series of separate 'points'.

Don't start with the words 'Another', 'Firstly', 'Secondly', etc.: one of my personal stylistic bugbears is the use of 'Another' at the beginning of paragraphs and sentences. I can see why it happens:

if a question asks you to 'Discuss the ways in which...' or 'How does ...', the obvious way to answer is with a series of 'ways'. So we have a first paragraph that explains one way in which a particular effect is achieved, followed by a second which begins '*Another* way in which...', followed by a third that begins the same way, and so on.

The problem with 'Another' is that it immediately makes an essay sound like a list rather than an argument. It also implies that the ideas expressed could really be in any order, whereas **your essay should have a necessary, logical and coherent order** whereby, ideally, each idea builds on, develops, qualifies or challenges the idea that precedes it.

Some students try to *imply* a structure by beginning paragraphs with 'Firstly', 'Secondly' etc.. First, as any good pedant will tell you, there is no need for an adverbial form of the ordinals (first, second, third) as these function as both adjective and adverb. And while you might go as far as 'fourthly', would you really say 'seventhly'? Also, 'numbering' your ideas in this way once again creates an impression that the essay is a list of discrete items rather than a single developing argument. And it's easy to lose count, as Dogberry, the foolish constable in *Much Ado About Nothing*, demonstrates:

Marry sir, they have committed false report, moreover they have spoken untruths, secondarily,

*they are slanders, sixth and lastly, they have belied
a lady, thirdly they have verified unjust things, and
to conclude, they are lying knaves.*

**Don't start with the words 'Lastly' or 'The final
way in which…':** The problem with these phrases is
that they imply that there is a finite number of 'ways'
in which a writer can and does achieve an effect.
Strictly speaking, that may be true, but it's not a
good idea to suggest that you have reached the end
of your possible answers when we reach the end of
your essay. If we begin a third paragraph by saying
'The final way in which Dickens makes Bounderby
a dislikeable character is by…', we imply that there
are *only* three ways in which Dickens achieves this
effect and that we have completed our job by
covering all of them and that there is no more to say.

The joy of intellectual life – and especially of
literary study – is that there is *always* more to say
and *no* answer is definitive. And even if you really
have only three things to say in response to the
question, others will have different ideas. Besides,
it's a good idea at least to imply that you could say
more had you space enough and time.

The paragraph

The rest of the paragraph is designed to provide
support for the idea expressed in the topic sentence.
This will come in the form of specific examples and
quotations, with a clear explanation of how and why

they back up the topic sentence's argument.

It's at this point that the essay really goes into textual detail and a good paragraph is likely to contain at least one significant quotation from a text. If I can risk yet another metaphor, the introduction, topic sentences and conclusion form the skeleton of an essay, while the quotation, evidence and analysis we find in each paragraph are the vital organs. Without those vital organs, the essay might have shape and structure, but it would be a) dead and b) rather too skinny.

You may have been taught to build paragraphs around a structure that some teachers call PQA (Point-Quotation-Analysis) and others PEA (Point-Example-Analysis) or, even more hilariously, PEE (Point-Evidence-Explanation). The latter can lead to advice such as 'Don't forget to PEE in the exam hall' or 'I couldn't find any PEE in your essay' or 'Your essay was full of PEE'. Be tolerant: teaching is a tough job. These things keep us going.

Rigid though it may seem, PQA/PEA/PEE is an excellent pattern to follow and produces strong, clear essays. A paragraph should be made up of a topic sentence, followed by enough PQA/PEA/PEE to convince the reader that what you've said in the topic sentence is sound and cogent.

Let's explore exactly what PQA/PEA/PEE means.

Point: I have a personal distaste for the use of the

word 'point' to mean 'idea' but I'm going to live with it for now. A 'point' is effectively a sentence expressing an important idea in your own words. You may wonder what makes it different from a topic sentence. The answer is that, in most cases, it's not the first sentence in a paragraph but the second. Unlike a topic sentence, it homes in on the actual text and prepares us for evidence or a quotation to back it up.

So while a topic sentence might make an assertion about the role of animals in *all* of Hardy's novels, the 'point' sentence might narrow the focus to animals in *Tess of the d'Urbervilles*.

Let's imagine that we're working on the essay question 'Discuss the ways in which Gerard Manley Hopkins's poetry explores the effects of modern industrial culture'.

In the paragraph we're building, we're going to discuss Hopkins's view of the ways in which industrialisation and industrialism affect the natural environment. So our topic sentence might read:

Hopkins tends to see modern industrial culture as a threat to the natural order and beauty of the environment.

We might follow this with a 'point' sentence which makes the reader focus on a particular aspect of a particular poem:

> Hopkins's awareness of this threat is perhaps most evident in 'Binsey Poplars', where the speaker laments the felling of a stand of trees near Oxford.

This is definitely not a topic sentence: the use of 'this threat' refers us to a previous sentence. There's also no reference back to the terms of the question as would be required in a topic sentence. The question asked us about all of Hopkins's poetry but this 'point' sentence narrows the focus and informs us that the next few lines – though not necessarily the whole paragraph – will be about the individual poem 'Binsey Poplars'.

Alternatively, a 'point' sentence might make a more specific observation about form, structure and language:

> Modern industrial culture is often described through violent vocabulary and imagery which present it as a threatening and polluting force.

A sentence such as this obviously demands to be followed immediately by some quoted and analysed examples.

Quotation/Example/Evidence: the 'point' sentence needs to be supported fully by evidence, whether in the form of factual information or quotation. We might feel that a single example is enough to support the point fully. So our sentence

Modern industrial culture is often described through violent vocabulary and imagery which present it as a threatening and polluting force

might be followed by this 'Quotation/example/evidence' sentence:

In 'Binsey Poplars', for example, Hopkins laments explicitly the way that in industrialised 19th century England 'we hack and rack the growing green'.

Or we might choose to present a series of quoted examples from different parts of a text, highlighting a particular pattern in the writer's language and imagery:

It is noticeable that in 'Binsey Poplars' Hopkins uses a range of violent verbs such as 'delve', 'hew', 'hack' and 'rack' to describe human interactions with the environment.

Or you might present a series of similar examples from a range of texts:

In a number of poems, Hopkins presents urban industrial culture as a taint or poison, describing its effects using verbs such as 'sours' ('Duns Scotus' Oxford'), 'seared', 'bleared', 'smeared' ('God's Grandeur').

Remember that, as in these examples, quotations must be properly blended into your sentence so that it makes sense. Don't just shove in a quotation to produce hideous nonsensical phrases such as:

> Hopkins uses violent imagery 'hack and rack the growing green'.

Analysis/Explanation: success in the third phase of the PQA/PEA/PEE process often distinguishes the very good essay from the merely competent one. It's important to recognise that **quotations do not speak for themselves**; you may know which part of the quotation is supporting the idea that you want to express but it may not be self-evident to your reader.

Analysis is the tricky bit but also the most satisfying, the moment where you can clinch an argument and demonstrate your skill as a close reader. The analysis sentence – or sentences, as you may need more than one – is where you tell the reader exactly what it is that you want him/her to notice in the quotation or example that you've just given. It's in this sentence that you'll point out technical features, patterns or contrasts in the quotation that you've just presented.

So I might follow my 'point' sentence

> Modern industrial culture is often described through violent vocabulary and imagery which present it as a threatening and polluting force

with the quotation/example/evidence sentence

> It is noticeable that in 'Binsey Poplars' Hopkins uses a range of violent verbs such as 'delve', 'hew', 'hack' and 'rack' to describe human interactions with the environment

then clinch the argument with the following close analysis:

> These are all violent actions which involve tools such as spades and axes and also suggest violence towards a human body, especially in the case of 'rack', which refers to a form of torture engine. The monosyllabic nature of these verbs and the use of guttural [k] endings creates a harsh, discordant sound, perhaps mimicking the axe-strokes that brought down the poplars and contrasting with the gentle sibilance used elsewhere in the poem to describe features of the '[s]weet especial rural scene'.

In these two sentences, we're really down in the greasy engine-room of a poem, working at the level of individual words and even sounds to show how a particular effect is created. It's the level of **detailed, analysed evidence** that you provide that makes the difference between mere assertion and genuine argument.

To see how the different phases of a paragraph work together to make a cogent argument, let's put them together in different colours, where the bold, black text is the topic sentence, orange is the Point, black-underline the Quotation/Example/Evidence and orange-underline the Analysis:

> **Hopkins tends to see modern industrial culture as a threat to the natural order and beauty of the environment.** Modern industrial culture is often described through violent vocabulary and imagery which present it as a threatening and polluting force. <u>In a number of poems, Hopkins presents urban industrial culture as a taint or poison, describing its effects using verbs such as 'sours' ('Duns Scotus' Oxford'), 'seared', 'bleared', 'smeared' ('God's Grandeur').</u> <u>These words all suggest the spoiling of something that was once pure, whether through burning ('seared') or sullying ('bleared', 'smeared'), reflecting the literal pollution of the environment by machinery and implying a more metaphorical corruption of the human spirit.</u>

We've worked only once through the PQA/PEA/PEE but already we have a fairly sizeable paragraph. It's up to you to decide how many times you need to repeat the process to make the idea in the topic sentence truly persuasive but I tend to find that three is about the maximum; any more, and there's a risk of unnecessary repetition and long, unwieldy paragraphs.

Chapter Five: The Conclusion

"Stupidity consists in wanting to reach conclusions."
Gustave Flaubert, letter to Louis Bouilhet, 4 September 1850

"Conclusions are the weak points of most authors, but some of the fault lies in the very nature of conclusion, which is at best a negation."
George Eliot, letter to John Blackwood, May 1857

"The anxiety, which in this state of their attachment must be the portion of Henry and Catherine, and of all who loved either, as to its final event, can hardly extend, I fear to the bosom of my readers, who will see in the tell-tale compression of the pages before them, that we are hastening together to perfect felicity."
Jane Austen, *Northanger Abbey*

"That's something the novelist can't help giving away, isn't it, that his book is coming to an end? It may not be a happy ending, nowadays, but he can't disguise the tell-tale compression of the pages... I mean, mentally you brace yourself for the ending of a novel. As you're reading, you're aware of the fact that there's only a page or two left in the book, and you get ready to close it."
David Lodge, *Changing Places*

'To conclude' is literally 'to close' or 'to shut'. We use the verb to describe the action of ending but it also has the meaning 'to arrive by reasoning at a judgement or opinion' (*OED*).

The conclusion of an essay does both of these things: it marks the ending and is the spot where writers gives their 'final' judgements or opinions on the question posed at the beginning. It's not a case of finally coming off the fence at this point – your introduction will have set out your view – but more of stating clearly and succinctly your 'final' answer to the question, though a conclusion is also a space where you can acknowledge that no answer is definitive and that your mind doesn't close just because your essay has to.

The conclusion is an important moment in an essay. It's the last thing a reader/examiner will read and, although your reader will have by this stage gained a clear impression of your overall grasp of the issue, it's always a good idea to bid a clear, neat, even elegant farewell. It would be fair to say that, especially in exams, a conclusion isn't a 'make or break' moment, but it's still one where we can leave a telling final impression and where the able student can deliver that clinching *coup de grâce*. Think about the literary texts you've read or films you love: a fluffed or fudged ending doesn't necessarily ruin an otherwise great work but it can leave you feeling disappointed.

It's surprising, though, how often conclusions of essays (like introductions) are left unplanned.

Many an otherwise detailed essay plan ends with the sub-heading 'Conc.' and a blank space. In exams, the conclusion is often a frantically scribbled afterthought rather than a crafted final flourish.

I suspect that students often feel that they will decide what goes in the conclusion when they get there. This seems to be rather like setting out on a holiday without knowing exactly where you're going or without a bed booked for the night.

So my first recommendation for conclusions is to **plan them**. Make sure your conclusion forms part of the essay plan you write before beginning.

Conclusions should be short: five to ten lines of average handwriting is enough. A conclusion is unlikely to include much quotation or close textual analysis, as the emphasis should be on an overview and an answer to the question. Often, a conclusion will begin with a phrase such as 'To conclude, ...', 'In conclusion, ...' or 'In summary, ...', which can serve as a useful marker of a move towards that more synoptic mode.

A conclusion should include a re-statement of your major argument, ideally in one sentence. Try to include words from the question, as in topic sentences, so that it is clear that you are answering the question directly. Obviously, there will be some element of repetition here; after all, you will have given a similar answer back in the introduction. But try to use slightly different phrasing. If your essay has followed a 'for-and-against' structure, make sure you acknowledge both sides but make it clear which you ultimately favour.

An effective way to do this is to set out your major argument in the main clause of the sentence, while acknowledging the 'other' side within a subordinate clause beginning with a subordinating conjunction such as 'Although', 'Though' or 'While'. Here are a few examples of appropriate first sentences for a concluding paragraph:

While it is certainly the case that Larkin depicts the harsh reality of many women's lives and shows genuine compassion for their sufferings, he repeatedly fails to allow women a voice in his poetry and seems at times to fall back on misogynistic stereotypes.

Although it can be argued that Richard II *is a play about the suffering and downfall of an individual, to do so is to fall for Richard's own self-mythology and to limit the play's political power and significance.*

Though it is certainly possible to see Waiting for Godot *as an Aristotelian tragedy, due to its focus on decline and its observation of dramatic unities, the play lacks the sense of final closure and catastrophe that would allow true catharsis to take place.*

A sentence such as this will certainly suffice as a conclusion, offering a neat closure to the argument and making a clear link back to the question, introduction and topic sentences. It may be all that you have time for in an exam. If you can, though, **try to follow your direct answer with something *new***, a slightly different perspective or take on the issue that you've been debating.

Some find this idea of adding something new in a conclusion a little alarming, fearing that it's late in the day to be embarking on a new tack and that any new argument will be unfinished and unsupported. In the best essays, however, the conclusion suggests strongly that the writer has plenty more to say if given more time and space.

Ideally, the essay should suggest that even at the end – and indeed beyond the end – *you are still thinking*. A good conclusion should give the message that 'my essay is ending but my thinking never will'. Although you're concluding, you're not closing down. This is, I think, what the French novelist Gustave Flaubert meant when he stated that stupidity "consists in wanting to reach conclusions". For Flaubert, the truly stupid man is the man with all the answers, who is satisfied that the world can be explained, summarised and finished off.

It is possible to introduce a new idea in a conclusion, or at least suggest that the thinking process doesn't end with the essay, in just a few words. A simple way to do this is to acknowledge an absence in your essay, a way of thinking about the question that you haven't had time to pursue but which the reader might like to consider. For example, you might think back to the terms of the question and consider alternative ways in which a key word or phrase could be interpreted.

> *In this essay, I have only considered Shakespeare's presentation of regime change in the political sphere. We could just as easily, however, argue that Shakespeare is as fascinated by 'regime change' in the home and shifts in domestic and familial power structures.*

Or you might acknowledge that your essay has focused exclusively on one character, and that the answer to the question would be different if we posed the same question about other characters:

> *It is nevertheless important to remember that Edward II is not the only king that we see in Marlowe's play. In the final scene of the play, his son Edward III has emerged as a model of a king who is decisive, dedicated and humane, suggesting that perhaps Marlowe does not reject entirely the institution of monarchy.*

Or you might suggest that the answer to the question would be very different if we answered it with a focus on another of the writer's works, or on a different period of his/her writing career:

> *However, while* Waiting for Godot *ultimately celebrates the mutually supportive partnership of Vladimir and Estragon, Beckett's later works seem*

*to attest to a certain loss of faith in the double act,
as plays such as* Krapp's Last Tape, Not I *and*
Rockaby *are the monologues of increasingly
isolated figures.*

Or you might re-consider the question in the light of
a piece of contextual material that you haven't
discussed before in the essay:

Although The Woman in White *ends with a scene
of apparent domestic bliss, the conventional family
in the novel is predominantly the site and means of
oppression, especially of women. Collins's attack
on the Victorian cult of the family was no doubt
inspired in part by his own unconventional
domestic circumstances: though never married to
Caroline Graves, he lived with her for most of his
life and also had two illegitimate children with
Martha Rudd. Collins's life was lived at least
partially outside the confines of Victorian
respectability and his novels delight in exposing
the secrets and miseries behind the façade of the
perfect middle-class family.*

It may seem risky to acknowledge 'omissions' or
'absences' at this late stage but I feel that the benefits
outweigh the risks. If you've written a clear, focused
essay, your reader will be familiar with your main
argument long before reaching the conclusion. After
a reminder of that main argument, isn't it worth
letting a little fresh air into the essay, demonstrating

that no argument is exhaustive, that no word is the last word, that to conclude is not to close? End on an opening – to the future, to the world, to the reader.

Chapter Six: Writing about a passage or poem

As we discussed earlier, some essay questions are about a passage of prose, drama or poetry. Many students feel instinctively reassured by the sight of a 'passage-based' question. Having a passage printed in front of you provides a kind of safety net; you can plunder the text for quotations and examples and the nuts and bolts of language and form are visibly present and available for analysis.

Everything that has been said so far in this book about interrogating the question, the planning process, the introduction, topic sentences, paragraphs and conclusions applies to the answering of passage-based questions. But there are a a few additional factors to bear in mind as you approach them.

Questioning the question

In a passage-based essay, the question should still be your starting point and the focus and filter for your reading of the passage. Remember that, like any essay, a passage-based essay must be an *argument*; it's not a paraphrase of the passage. The question, as we have seen, is your greatest aid to structuring an argument and so it pays to consider the question, interrogate it and bear it in mind throughout.

The format of passage-based questions varies but there are certain recurring patterns.

1. Questions that ask you to write about the presentation of an individual character or relationship in the passage

> *How does Milton present the relationship between Adam and Eve in this passage?*
>
> *Explore Miller's presentation of Eddie's relationship with Catherine in this extract.*

These are the most straightforward passage-based questions. To make sure there is a sense of development to your argument, try to think about different (and ideally contrasting) ways in which a character or relationship is presented. So we might look first at ways in which the Eddie/Catherine relationship is presented as mutually supportive and affectionate, before turning to look at ways in which tension and mutual irritation are suggested, before turning to look at ways in which the relationship appears disturbing and even abusive.

2. Questions that ask you to write about the

> *Discuss the ways in which the poet explores the effects of growing old.*
> *Explore how Coleridge gives a vivid sense of the effects of solitude in this extract from 'The Rime of the Ancient Mariner'*

Again, the most important step to answering such a question is to be flexible in your thinking and to examine the theme from more than one angle. So, the question 'Discuss the ways in which the poet explores the effects of growing old' might be answered by looking first at how the physical effects of growing old are described, then at the emotional effects. Or we might look at how the poet presents the negative aspects of growing old, before turning to look at the more positive aspects of ageing.

3. Questions that ask you to consider how a writer makes a passage dramatic/revealing/ significant/ amusing/moving/memorable

> *How does Priestley's writing make this such a dramatic and significant moment in the play?*
>
> *How does Wells's writing make this such a gripping opening to the novel?*

These questions are really asking you to look closely at the writer's language and technique and their effect on a reader or audience. Once again, it's important to make sure your essay *develops*, so it's worth aiming to think about more than one way in which a writer achieves his or her effects.

The danger is that 'adjective' questions like the ones above can lead inquisitive students into rather arid reflections on exactly what is meant by the adjective in question. I'm not convinced that those who set questions always reflect as deeply on the meanings of these words as they should. To save you from becoming lost in such speculation, here's my own glossary:

- **dramatic** = likely to create a strong response in an audience or reader. Strong responses include shock, excitement, suspense, fear, anger, pity, sorrow. Dramatic effect can be inherent in a situation (e.g. an argument, a death, a birth, a reunion, a farewell) and/or (more importantly) it can be created and heightened by the language used by narrators and characters and by the techniques of a writer.
- **significant** = important in the development of a character, relationship or plot. 'Significant' moments have a profound effect on the rest of the story or on a character's later life or on the subsequent course of a relationship. So the first or last meeting of two major characters is significant, as is the first or last time the audience or reader meets a character.
- **revealing** = telling us something we didn't know

before. Typically, a moment where we see a previously unknown side of a character is 'revealing'. So a soliloquy might reveal to us that a character we had previously thought to be a thoroughly good egg is in fact an utter swine.

- **amusing/comic/humorous** = likely to make an audience or reader laugh. There's always the student who says (usually about Shakespeare): 'But I didn't find it funny'. For the purposes of the essay, especially in an exam, pretend that you *did* find it funny or break the confines of your own purblind soul and consider why *someone else* might find it funny. A useful way to approach questions that ask you about humour is to think about the inherent comedy of the situation (e.g. a man being mistaken for someone else, a woman having to pretend to her husband that she is alone when we and she know her lover is in the wardrobe), linguistic comedy (e.g. puns, hyperbole, malapropisms) and physical comedy (e.g. falling over, wearing ass's ears, wearing a coat that's much too small etc.)
- **moving** = likely to make a reader or audience feel sad, pitiful, tender. Again, situations themselves can be moving (farewells, deaths, reunions) but you should focus more on the ways in which the writer's linguistic and technical decisions heighten the emotional punch of the passage.
- **memorable** = all of the above, but perhaps closest to 'dramatic' and 'significant'. I think we could say that 'memorable' means 'likely to have

a lasting impact on a reader or audience'. It does not, as one of my students once thought, mean 'easy to memorise'.

4. 'Critical commentary' questions

These are rather old-fashioned nowadays but they do still appear, especially at university level. The wording can be as terse as:

> *Write a critical commentary on the following passage.*

> *Write a critical appreciation of the following passage, commenting on the writer's language, style and form.*

These questions offer you no real steer or prompt on how to focus your essay and so you have to do more of the heavy lifting yourself. On the other hand, you have total freedom to choose what aspects of the passage you study. Ideally, you should aim to concentrate on *three* major areas, which will form the stages or phases of your argument.

5. Comparison questions

Sometimes you will be given two poems or passages and asked to compare them. You may be invited to look the way in which they consider a particular theme:

Compare the ways in which relationships between mothers and daughters are presented in these two poems.

Or you may be asked to write about one specific poem and another of your choice:

Discuss the ways in which Rossetti writes about women's lives in 'Passing and Glassing' and one other poem.

Or you may be given a rather terse invitation:

Write a critical comparison of the following poem and prose extract.

Though opinions vary on the best way to structure comparison essays, I am strongly in favour of dealing with the two texts together as much as possible, rather than treating each separately. The text-by-text approach militates against effective comparison, can become repetitive and tends to mean that one of the texts (usually the one discussed second) is liable to get fairly short shrift, especially under timed conditions.

I favour looking at how *both* texts present different aspects of a theme (or different themes) in each paragraph. Each topic sentence should mention both texts, ideally identifying a major similarity and/or difference between them and every paragraph should deal with both texts. There is no need to give exactly the same amount of attention to both, but make sure one text doesn't become too dominant. Don't mention the 'second' text only at the end of paragraphs. Such an approach makes comparison only one-way and tends to relegate one text to a secondary role.

6. 'Feelings' questions

There's a type of question which asks you to consider how a writer expresses/conveys/communicates his/her feelings about a particular theme or person.

> *Discuss the ways in which Clarke expresses her feelings for her daughter in 'Catrin'.*

> *How does the writer vividly convey his emotions on the death of his mother?*

If faced with one of these 'feelings' questions, always **identify the emotions expressed**. This can be done in the first sentence of your introduction. And try to **identify more than one emotion**. Remember that humans are complex and capable of experiencing more than one emotion simultaneously. Indeed, arguably it is the need to cope with mixed and indeed conflicting emotions that drives people to the production of creative art. More pragmatically, identifying more than one emotion will ensure that your essay has a structure and a sense of development, with each of the emotions you identify forming the subject of a paragraph.

So we might answer one of the questions above by beginning our introduction with the sentence:

In 'Catrin', Clarke explores a mother's strong feelings of affection towards her daughter but also acknowledges the tensions and conflicts between them, as well as expressing a combination of fear and admiration of her daughter's growing independence.

7. Climbing the scaffolding

Once upon a time, exam questions were almost telegrammatic in their no-nonsense succinctness. We'd usually get a statement followed by the single word 'Discuss'. Or take this example from a Cambridge A Level English Literature paper in June 1957: 'Estimate the significance of Peacock as a critic of the Romantic movement'. This was the educational equivalent of being handed a parachute and pushed out of a plane over Berlin with the words 'Good luck, old boy'.

Nowadays, examiners are much more sensitive and enlightened, realising that exams should create the optimal circumstances for a student to succeed (either that, or these snowflakes require much gentler handling and don't know they've been born harrumph harrumph...) For whatever reason, examiners have grown more generous and garrulous, to the point where exam questions are now sometimes mini-essays themselves. In particular, recent years have seen the emergence of what we might term supplementary instructions or 'scaffolding'. These instructions usually come after the question itself and give you a more or less clear idea of how you might like to go about the task. Sometimes these instructions come in the same sentence as the question:

> *Write a critical commentary on the following passage, considering in detail the ways in which your responses are shaped by the writer's choice of form, structure and language.*

This isn't much help, as any decent literary essay is going to do those things anyway. Some instructions, however, are more specific and come in the form of a list of bullet-pointed list things that you 'might like' to include:

> *How does the poet express his feelings on the birth of his son?*
> *To help you answer the question, you might consider:*
>
> * *the ways in which he describes his son's body*
> * *his description of his own emotions*
> * *how his feelings develop in the last stanza*

The golden rule when faced when one of these little essay menus is to **follow the bullet points,** in the order in which they appear in the question. They aren't the gentle suggestions they appear to be; it's better to treat them as commands. If you follow them, you've got your three main paragraphs. And it's not a bad idea to use some of the words of each of the bullet points in your topic sentences.

The introduction

All of the advice on introductions in Chapter Four holds good for passage-based essays. There are, however, a couple of additional, important features which help to make a clear, confident beginning to a passage-based essay:

A one-sentence summary of what happens in the passage/poem and what it is about: offering a clear overview of the whole text at this stage will help to clarify your own thoughts and suggest that you have a confident command of the text that you're facing. Just a single sentence at the very beginning of the introduction will do. If there's a narrative element to the passage or poem, give a very brief summary of what occurs within it. In addition, give a very brief idea of what the major theme or subject of the text is. So we might open with something like this:

In this passage, Silas goes to look at his beloved gold and discovers, to his utter horror and dismay, that, as the reader already knows, it has been stolen from its hiding-place.

Or

> *In 'The Relic', Donne imagines the future disinterment of his skeleton and the future grave-digger's possible responses to the bracelet of his lover's hair that he will wear when he is dead, which leads Donne into reflection on how subsequent generations might treat their remains as sacred relics, before stating how he would like them to be viewed.*

This summary sentence should be as brief as possible; a full paraphrase of the text is unnecessary and undesirable. It should be followed by a one-sentence direct answer to the question. So if the question about the passage where Silas Marner discovers the theft of his gold were 'How does Eliot make this passage such a dramatic and significant moment in *Silas Marner*?' we might follow the summary sentence with

> *Eliot makes this such a dramatic moment through her adoption of Silas's perspective, by her hyperbolic descriptions of his physical and emotional reactions and by using the empty hole in his floor as a metaphor for his empty life.*

If you're writing about an extract from a longer piece of poetry, prose or drama, it's essential to set the passage in context in your introduction. By 'context' here, I mean the context of the larger narrative. So you should explain where this passage fits into the broader story. So in no more than one or two sentences, state what's just happened, why this is a significant moment – Does it mark the first or last meeting of two characters? Is it our first encounter with a major character? Is it a turning-point in the story? – and how it will affect subsequent events:

> *In the previous chapter, we have seen Dunstan Cass steal Silas's gold, and so there is great tension and dramatic irony here as we know the shock that awaits Silas. Although the theft seems to be a disaster to Silas and the reader at this point, by the end of the novel we realise that this theft is in fact a blessing in disguise, as it brings Silas into contact with the Raveloe community and the removal of his gold deprives him of the object of his idolatrous and destructive love, leaving a space that will be filled by true love for Eppie.*

Contextualising in this way not only demonstrates a confident knowledge of the whole text, but will often enable you to identify significant features of a passage that rely for their effect on a relationship with previous or subsequent events.

For example, Romeo and Juliet's dawn parting in Act 3, Scene 5, is all the more moving, ironic and dramatically effective when we know that this is the last time that they will speak to one another and see one another 'alive'. (The next time that Romeo sees

Juliet in Act 5, Scene 3, he thinks that she is dead and so poisons himself, not knowing that she is in fact merely in a drug-induced sleep.)

Structure

When writing about a passage or poem, it may seem logical to write a line-by-line 'commentary'. It is, however, unwise to do so. There are several reasons why I do not favour the line-by-line (or paragraph-by-paragraph or stanza-by-stanza) approach, some of which are purely practical and some of which are more related to the fundamentals of how a text works. It simply isn't economical to write a line-by-line analysis of a text.

In practice, if you adopt a line-by-line approach, it's almost inevitable, especially under time pressure, that the first lines of the poem or extract will receive far more attention than the latter half, which is liable to receive short shrift as your energy declines and/or the 'stop writing now please' moment draws near. This could be disastrous, as it's not impossible that those last lines may include some of the most important features of the poem or extract.

Line-by-line is also utterly predictable and, frankly, boring: once your reader knows that you're writing a line-by-line analysis, he or she knows exactly what's coming next. It's surely better to surprise your reader with a new angle in each paragraph than to embark on a dogged trudge through a text. Above all, a line-by-line approach is flawed because literature simply doesn't work in a linear, cumulative fashion.

One of the joys of literary analysis is tracing the many internal echoes, patterns, foreshadowings and contrasts within a single text. In order to see, hear and explain these, we need to step back and look at the text as a whole. Discussing each line, sentence or paragraph in isolation and in sequence will not enable us or the reader to experience the effect of a passage or poem, which is, after all, what you are asked to write about.

The best way to approach a passage-based essay is in a similar fashion to the way we approach other essays – by looking to construct a multi-phase argument that develops and looks at a text in different ways. So if asked to write about a passage, why not devote a paragraph to the ways in which a character is described, another to the ways in which a particular technique or group of images is used, another to the contrasts in linguistic tone and register in different parts of the extract? Above all, of course, **answer the question**. In passage-based essays as much as whole-text essays, the precise structure and content of your essay will be largely dictated by the question.

Notes

Notes

CG CONNELL GUIDES

Concise, intelligent guides to history and literature

CONNELL GUIDES TO LITERATURE

Novels and poetry

Emma

Far From the Madding Crowd

Frankenstein

Great Expectations

Hard Times

Heart of Darkness

Jane Eyre

Lord of the Flies

Mansfield Park

Middlemarch

Mrs Dalloway

Paradise Lost

Persuasion

Pride and Prejudice

Tess of the D'Urbervilles

The Canterbury Tales

The Great Gatsby

The Poetry of Robert Browning

The Waste Land

To Kill A Mockingbird

Wuthering Heights

Shakespeare

A Midsummer Night's Dream

Antony and Cleopatra

Hamlet

Julius Caesar

King Lear

Macbeth

Othello

Romeo and Juliet

The Second Tetralogy

The Tempest

Twelfth Night

Modern texts

A Doll's House

A Room with a View

A Streetcar Named Desire

An Inspector Calls

Animal Farm

Atonement

Beloved

Birdsong

Hullabaloo

Never Let Me Go

Of Mice and Men

Rebecca

Spies

The Bloody Chamber

The Catcher in the Rye

The History Boys

The Road

Vernon God Little

Waiting for Godot